PHYSICAL THERAPISTS

PEOPLE WHO CARE FOR OUR HEALTH

Robert James

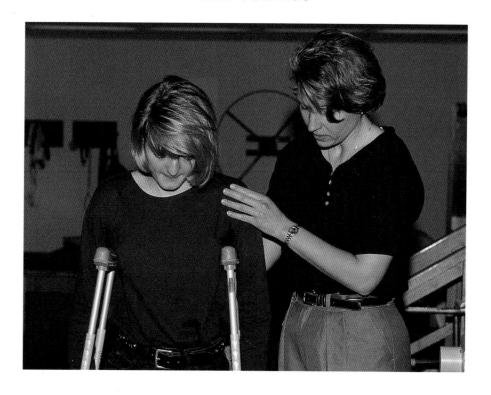

The Rourke Book Co., Inc.
Vero Beach, Florida 32964

PHOTO CREDITS
All photos © Kyle Carter except page 10 © Frank Sileman/Rainbow

ACKNOWLEDGEMENTS
The author thanks Sports Med, Carol Stream, IL and the Physical
Therapy Department of Mercy Center, Aurora, IL for their
cooperation in the publication of this book

Library of Congress Cataloging-in-Publication Data

James, Robert, 1942-
    Physical therapists / by Robert James.
        p. cm. — (People who care for our health)
    Includes index.
    Summary: Describes what physical therapists do, where they
work, and how they train and prepare for their jobs.
    ISBN 1-55916-170-1
    1. Physical therapy—Vocational guidance—Juvenile literature.
[1. Physical therapy—Vocational guidance. 2. Occupations.
3. Vocational guidance.]
I. Title II. Series: James, Robert, 1942- People who care for our
health
RM705.J35 1995
615.8'2'023—dc20
                                         95–18937
                                            CIP
                                            AC

Printed in the USA

TABLE OF CONTENTS

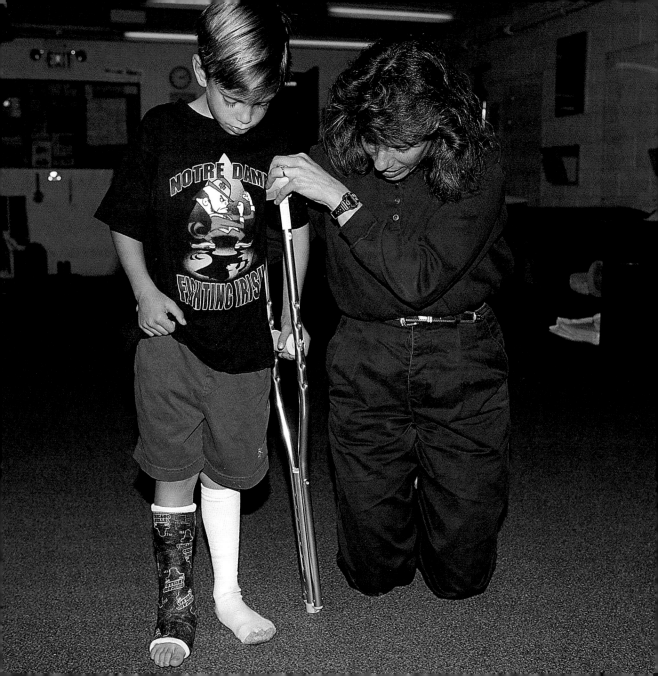

PHYSICAL THERAPISTS

Physical therapists (PT's) are the highly trained people who perform physical **therapy** (THER uh pee).

Physical therapy is a type of treatment for the body. It uses such physical means as cold, heat, and exercise to help **patients** (PAY shents).

Patients are the people whom PT's treat. Physical therapy patients are usually suffering from a certain disease or injury.

PT's often help patients heal, feel better, gain strength, and regain the use of body parts.

WHAT PHYSICAL THERAPISTS DO

Physical therapists treat patients of all ages. These patients have a variety of physical problems. Some patients have pain caused by diseases, such as arthritis, cancer, or muscular dystrophy.

PT's work with patients who have hurt their backs, arms, or legs. Many of these patients are athletes.

PT's also work with people who need to regain strength after an operation. Now and then, PT's work with healthy patients who simply want to improve their abilities.

A physical therapist straps a patient's foot into an exercise machine

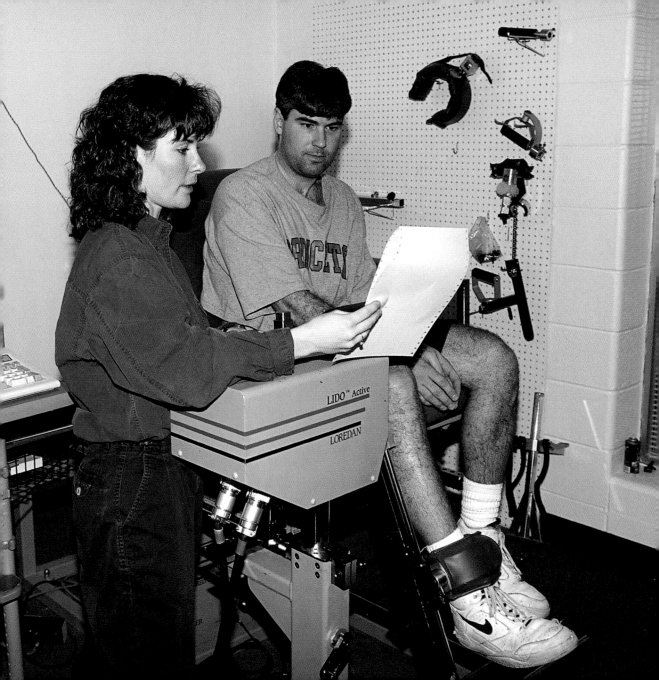

WHAT'S WRONG?

A physical therapist cannot help until he or she knows the patient's problem. Many problems of PT patients have already been determined by doctors. A PT, however, talks at length with each new patient and performs simple tests.

A physical therapist, for example, commonly checks the strength and range of movement of an injured arm or leg.

A physical therapist discusses with a patient the results of muscle testing done by this machine, which can also strengthen muscles

SPECIAL PATIENTS

Patients with **paralysis** (per AL uh sis) can be a special challenge for physical therapists. Paralysis causes the loss of feeling, often in arms or legs, and the loss of movement. **Strokes** (STROKES) and certain diseases and injuries can cause paralysis.

Physical therapists help people with paralysis try to regain the use of their limbs.

PT's also teach people how to use **artificial** (art uh FISH ul) arms and legs if they lose their own.

A physical therapist helps a stroke victim learn to walk

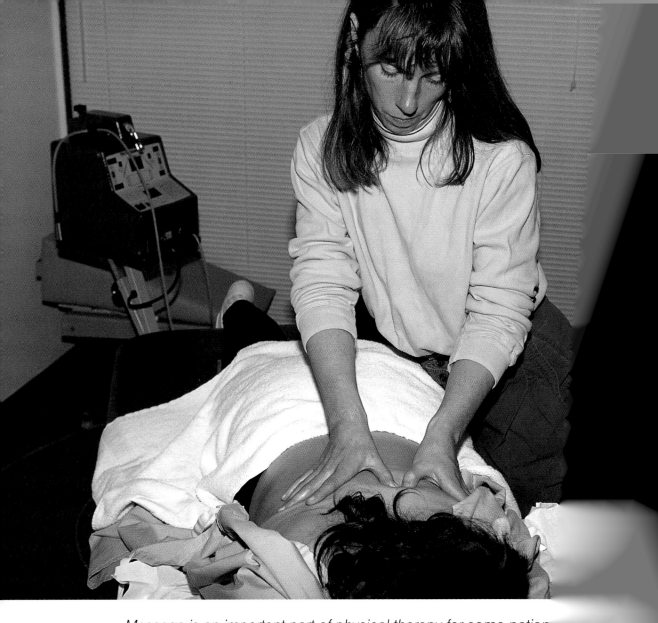

Massage is an important part of physical therapy for some patients.

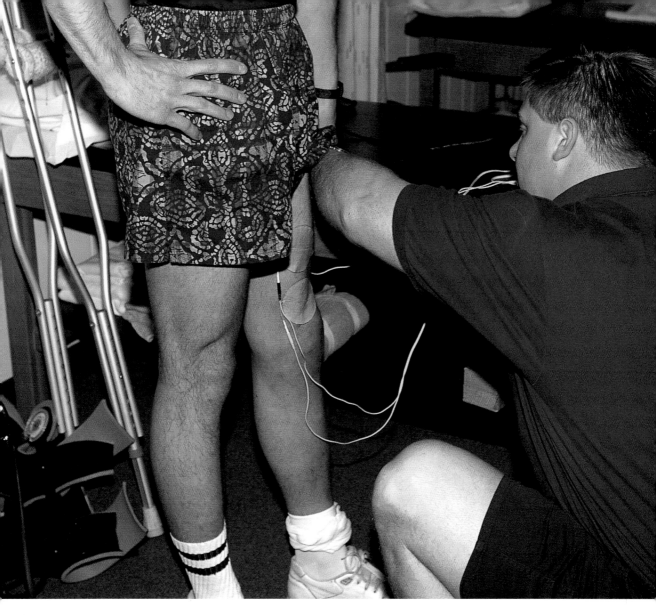

A physical therapist attaches an electric muscle stimulator machine to help strengthen a knee after surgery

HELPING PATIENTS

A physical therapist, with carefully controlled exercises, can help many patients. Exercises can strengthen muscles and improve a patient's range of movement. Exercise also helps some patients improve their balance.

Exercises may be performed by the patient alone or with a PT's help. A physical therapist may help a patient stretch an arm or leg to new limits.

Stretching tubes are used for strengthening several muscle groups

TREATMENTS

PT's have several ways, other than exercise, to treat patients. One method is the use of water in warm whirlpool baths. Swirling whirlpool currents often relax stiff and painful joints.

PT's use heat and cold treatments on certain patients. Ice packs can reduce swelling, and heating pads can ease pain.

Massage (muh SAHJ) is another type of physical therapy. A PT massages a group of muscles by rubbing, pushing, or squeezing them. Massage helps loosen tight muscles.

A physical therapy patient's ankle undergoes whirlpool therapy

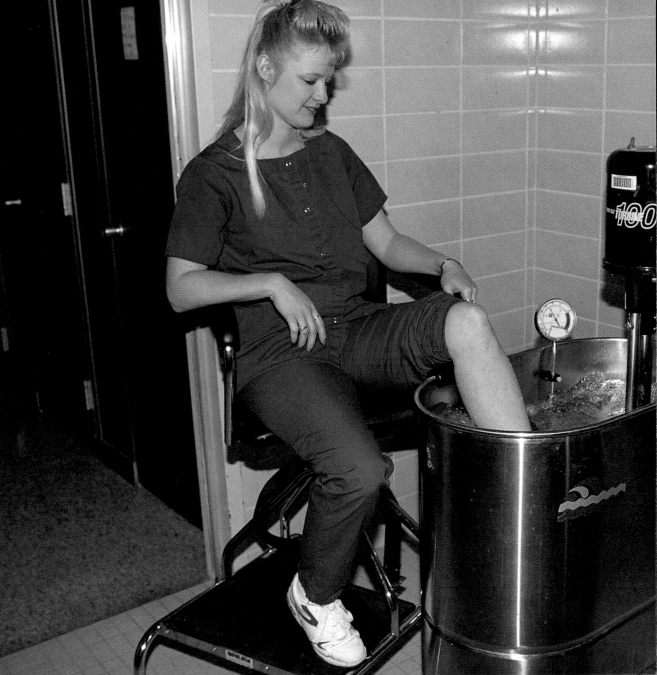

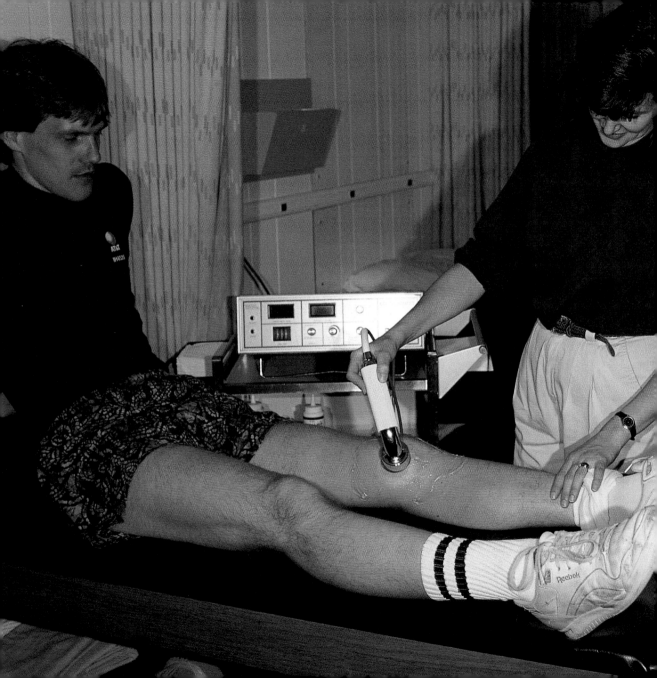

WHERE PHYSICAL THERAPISTS WORK

Physical therapists work in places where they have space and equipment to treat patients. Many PT's work in hospitals or clinics that have large areas set aside for physical therapy.

Some PT's travel to work in homes, schools, hospital rooms, and adult care centers. Other PT's work by themselves in private **practice** (PRAHK tiss).

A physical therapist applies the sound head of an ultrasound machine that will speed healing of the patient's knee

A PHYSICAL THERAPIST'S HELPERS

Physical therapists and other health care **professionals** (pro FESH un ulz) work together as a team to help patients return to normal, or near-normal, activity.

A doctor, for example, often refers patients to physical therapists. The doctor decides what's wrong with a patient and whether physical therapy might help.

Other health care workers help physical therapy patients prepare for normal daily living. These workers can reteach basic skills, like bathing or speaking.

Students of physical therapy learn about the body's muscles and bones

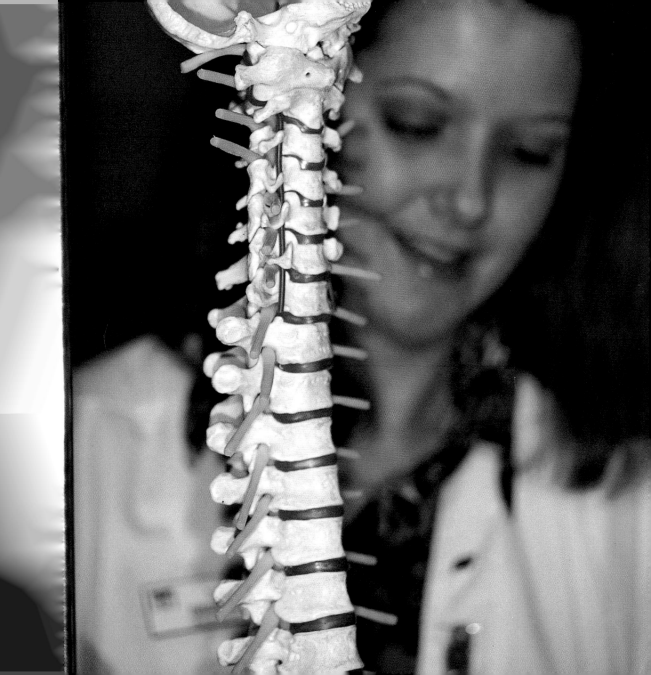

BECOMING A PHYSICAL THERAPIST

Physical therapists learn many of their special skills in college classes. A physical therapist must have at least a Bachelor's Degree in physical therapy to practice. Many PT's continue their studies beyond a basic degree from a four-year college.

Every American physical therapist must pass a state test before practicing as a physical therapist.

Glossary

artificial (ART uh FISH ul) — something human-made, but often similar to the natural thing in form and use

massage (muh SAHJ) — the use of hands to rub muscles for healthful purposes

paralysis (per AL uh sis) — loss of the ability to move

practice (PRAHK tiss) — the professional's private business

patients (PAY shents) — people treated by a physical therapist or other health-caregiver

professional (pro FESH un ul) — one who is highly trained, highly skilled, and paid for his or her work

stroke (STROKE) — a sudden break in a blood vessel of the brain, often causing some paralysis

therapy (THER uh pee) — treatment of a health problem

INDEX